BANFF & JASPER

THE SPLENDID NATIONAL PARKS

A pictorial guide to the spectacular World Heritage Sites

TEXT AND PHOTOGRAPHS BY
GEORGE BRYBYCIN

GB PUBLISHING

How fortunate we are in Canada with so many large and gorgeous national parks. Coupled with our country's low-density population, we are blessed with a high quality and standard of life. The very concept of 'national parks' arose in the United States where Yellowstone National Park was born. Canada's first park was created in 1885 around Banff's Sulphur Hot Springs. Enlarged several times to today's size of 6,641 sq. km. Jasper National Park came to life in 1907. It is the largest of five Rocky Mountain National Parks and comprises 10,878 sq. km. These two largest national parks of the Rockies are surrounded by Kootenay and Yoho National Parks and several Wilderness and Provincial Parks. To the south, by the U.S. border, little Waterton Lakes National Park is only "a bit larger" than New York's Central Park. Combined, all these parks protect about 40% of the south-central Rockies. The day is yet to come when Waterton Park is substantially enlarged and a new Tornado National Park north of highway 3 is created which would ensure that the Rockies along the Great Divide are all protected. Wildlife could then move freely north or south, keeping herds healthy and eliminating inbreeding which now occurs because small herds are isolated from each other.

A fragrant and eye-pleasing alpine garden of humble mountain flowers.

BANFF NATIONAL PARK

The Park is located along a major transportation corridor: Trans-Canada Highway and Canadian Pacific Railway. Both have traffic volume growth of about 8-10% a year which contributes to the deaths of hundreds of animals. Twinning the highway to the British Columbia border will bring a fenced road which will save many of those animals. Banff Park has several world famous attractions, such as emerald Lake Louise with monumental glaciated Mt. Victoria. Moraine Lake in the Valley of the Ten Peaks is an alpine paradise of first magnitude. The monumental 3,543 m high Mt. Temple looks down at the valley as the undisputed monarch of the area. Only Mt. Assiniboine and Mt. Forbes are higher in the Park. Northwest along highway 93 are located great glacial lakes: Hector, Bow, Caldron, Peyto, Mistaya, two Waterfowl Lakes and Chephren Lake. Most are fed by a large body of ice, namely Wapta Icefield. High glaciated and challenging mountains further grace this splendid area.

Further to the north the Glacier Lake area is another alpine paradise with the spectacular Mt. Forbes Group, Mt. Freshfield and five peaks of Mt. Lyell, where ice and snow reign, as this is high country. Close by to the north, huge Mt. Wilson sprawls on 30 sq. km featuring a large icefield on the north side. The northwest boundary of the Park is touching on eternal winter, the frozen world of the Columbia Icefield. Banff Park is primarily dominated by great coniferous forests of pine, spruce and fir. Along the lower valley, broadleaf trees can be found. At the timberline, here and there one can admire large stands of Lyell's Larch trees, especially in autumn when Larch needles turn yellow-gold. The northern limit of Larches is on the south side of Hector Lake. At the higher valleys and plateaus, gorgeous alpine meadows provide an impressive, dazzling, and colourful palette of flowers, particularly in July and August. Plants and herbs furnish a rich habitat for rodents and birds. Fauna is also diverse, plentiful and beautiful. Large mammals include: Moose, Caribou, Elk, Black and Whitetail Deer, Goat and Sheep. There are predatory carnivores such as Grizzly and Black Bear (omnivorous), Wolf, Wolverine, Coyote, Fox, Cougar, Lynx, Bobcat, Badger, and a few species of Weasel. Also common are Hare and Porcupine. Raptors – birds of prey, such as the Bald and Golden Eagles, Falcons, Owls, fish-eating Osprey, three species of Jay, Raven, Crow, and Magpie, as well as dozens of small birds are plentiful. Snakes do not inhabit the Park, except in a few locations where a harmless water snake may be found.

Banff Park can be rated as having a temperate climate, where summers are warm or even hot. Winter, especially in recent years, is not as cold as it used to be due to global warming. January can be a bit nippy; the other months are quite pleasant for skiing, skating, and building a snowman. Snowfall is abundant on the Great Divide and west of it. On the east side, it is just moderate. Banff Park, easily accessible by car, train, and air (Calgary International Airport) is home to three large, superb ski areas, where visitors from around the globe enjoy powder skiing for over six months annually. Nordic skiers also find unlimited trails throughout the Park. Alberta highways are well-maintained year-round and the resort towns of Banff, Lake Louise and Jasper, can satisfy the most discriminating jet-set tourist with world-class facilities and services.

A principal landmark of Banff Park – Castle Mountain (2766m), reflected in a pond along the Bow River, is a hiker and climber paradise, accessible by a comfortable all-seasons trail of intermediate grade. Carry plenty of water on a hot summer day and enjoy.

Bow Lake and surroundings is nothing short of a mountain paradise, easily accessible by car, along Lake Louise – Jasper Icefields Parkway. To the south sprawls huge Wapta Icefield. Its Bow Glacier gives birth to the blue-green Bow River.

Above: Would you rather sleep in a tent or an igloo? The latter is warmer and quieter –wind will not rattle it, and it takes only one hour to build. It could be -20°C outside but with the 'door' closed, the trapped air inside hovers at around zero. A candle may raise the temperature by five degrees. Location – near Lake Louise.

Left: Elk Crossing or Ford. Animals ford the rivers and lakes year-round, except during early summer run-off when water levels are dangerously high, even for swimmers like Moose and Elk. Supposedly all animals can swim, some however do it only when they have to. Bear, wild dogs, and cats, would rather not wet their fancy 'fur coats'. Bow River just west of Banff.

Above: The fun of horse riding increases in direct proportion to the attractiveness of the trail and terrain. In the Rockies, a number of spectacular rides are available, a few remote camps with food and accommodation also exist, a lifetime experience. Crossing Spray and Bow Rivers confluence.

Left: Not exactly a birds-eye view of Lower Waterfowl Lake, but almost. The author scrambled as high as possible, up the hill north of the Lake to capture this splendid image. Howse Peak (3290m) is in the middle and below it nests emerald Chephren Lake. Truly an alpine paradise.

The northeast face of Mt. Patterson (3197m) with Bluebird Glacier. Only ice and rock experts need apply; this is a 15-hour plus climb, if all goes well. From the south and west, easier routes do exist, but fording icy water and a glacier walk are involved. First scaled in 1924 by F.V. Field and W.O. Field, guided by E. Feuz.

Mt. Wilson (3261m), a massive mountain of many faces, ascent routes, and difficulties. The north side of the mountain is nothing but icefield, all with icefalls, crevasses and surprises as ice changes from year to year. The mountain is a major Goat habitat and the east slope is ablaze with colour in autumn.

Moraine Lake needs no introduction; most mountain enthusiasts have seen it many times - absolutely spectacular. Once upon a time a large rock slide blocked the creek and Moraine Lake was born. Its colour came from the presence of rock flour from nearby peaks, transported to the Lake by glacial meltwater. The area boasts of hiking trails, climbing routes, and...even a few resident Grizzly Bears. Caution is advised.

Cirque Lake is one of six glacial lakes along upper Mistaya River. All are fed by glacial meltwaters and feature gorgeous emerald waters whose colour intensity depends on season, temperature – ice melting. How do you get here? A half decent trail commences between Lower and Upper Waterfowl Lakes, but ends at the Lake. The author followed the torturous west shore and scrambled west to a col on his way to Chephren Lake's south end.

Above: There are three ways to see the Rockies: from the shoulder of the highway, hike up the valley, or climb a mountain. Here a climber admires Boom Glacier and its moraines, Boom Lake, and Larches of autumn – the high country as seen from Mt. Bell (2910m). Danger is involved here. For one who displays any symptoms of vertigo, staying in the valley is strongly advised.

Left: A rugged foreground with a beautiful and inspiring background. Looking south from Caldron Peak (2917m), on the left stands Peyto Peak (2970m), a distant icy giant at the centre is Mt. Baker (3172m) flanking the west end of Wapta Icefield. Caldron Lake graces this exceptional early morning image. Located southwest of Peyto Lake and accessible by alpine route, in some sections difficult.

A dominant elevation in the central Rockies, Mt. Temple (3543m) graces the horizon between Lake Louise and Moraine Lake – a fine alpine area. On the right stands of golden Larches decorate Little Temple. In the foreground, the low-level Bow River flows towards the Prairies. Despite its severe look, an average fit scrambler could ascend Mt. Temple, weather permitting.

A less conditioned hiker would require one and a half hours to reach Lake Agnes, while a fit one could do it in one hour. The Lake is west of Lake Louise, accessible by a wide and excellent trail. From here one can hike to higher vantage points and enjoy remarkable scenery. On the left is Devils Thumb (2458m) from where the author produced photo #20; on the right stands Three Needles (2590m) and far right features Mt. Whyte (2983m).

Above: Classic Banff, Mt. Rundle (2998m), autumnish and pretty as always, reflects its western face in mirror-like Vermilion Lake. Located next to the bustling tourist Mecca of Banff, the ecosystems of both mountain and lake appear to be undisturbed. The key to all ecological successes is awareness and education. If we want National Parks and Wilderness areas, we must treat our ecosystems with utmost respect.

Left: This photo features Sawback Range west of Banff, beautifully rugged and not easily accessible. Here in the Valley, autumn is just approaching. A solitary wild Gooseberry bush exhibits its seasonally gorgeous hues. Distant poplars show little sign of turning gold, still displaying rich green leaves. Grass is ready for its blanket of white fluff, as the darkened sky portrays sure signs of the season. "For everything there is a season".

The unique scenery from Devils Thumb (2458m). On the left is Lake Agnes, centre Big Beehive (2255m), and to the right Lake Louise. In the distance "beautiful signs of civilization" are evident. An attractive and enjoyable area with many short hikes and scrambles available.

Peyto Lake and area is wild; Bill Peyto, after whom the Lake is named, is widely known as "Wild Bill". Bill was an early guide and packer and loved life and fun on the wild side. The Lake is located southwest of Bow Summit on Icefields Parkway and is photographed here from the ridge south of the Lake.

Above: A first sign of approaching spring, the breakup of the ice on the Bow River after a lengthy, sometimes harsh, Canadian winter. Craggy and monumental Castle Mountain (2766m) stands patiently anxiously awaiting pleasant summer days when many people will come to visit good old Castle.

Left: If you like fast-changing, unpredictable weather, the Bow Lake is the place to be. Immediate proximity to the Great Divide and large Wapta Icefield does it. It is circa five degrees colder here, with wind and precipitation higher as well. Crowfoot Mountain (3050m) basks in the rising sun as Bow Lake is shrouded in the morning mist.

The lake of many moods, colours and features – the one and only Lake Louise. This emerald jewel of the Rockies is the most-visited lake in Canada, a must see place. Located approximately 55 km west of Banff near the Trans-Canada Highway, the area is a haven for hikers, climbers and artists.

Nothing short of a mountain paradise: Mt. Chephren (3266m), glacial-green Lower Waterfowl Lake, lush healthy forest and cobalt-blue Alberta sky. It took little effort to scramble up the walls north of the Lake to produce this splendid image. Per ardua ad astra, *as the Romans would say.*

Above: Skiing is here to stay. It tripled and quadrupled in the number of participants in the last 25 years. A few high level cross-country races are held annually in the Rockies. The 1988 Olympic legacy, Canmore Nordic Centre, helps promote this phenomenally healthy and elegant sport. Here a few hundred racers dash on Lake Louise for fame, glory and healthy exercise in an annual event.

Left: From a humble beginning, in a few decades, Canada has become a middle power in alpine skiing. Ten large major ski areas prosper in the Rockies alone. It is an exquisite and expensive sport but certainly healthier than a noisy, smoky bar. Ski touring and ascending a mountain on skis is a huge thrill, except for the ever-present avalanche danger. Enjoy, but know what you are doing! The photo features the grand Lake Louise Ski Area.

Bow Summit along Icefields Parkway is known for its many features: great green lakes, lush forests, home to the Grizzly Bear and other fauna. Flora, however, is something extra special here. South of the summit above the treeline, gorgeous flowery meadows sprawl along the north slopes of Mt. Jimmy Simpson (2970m). Large varieties of flowers can be seen as early as June, poking through the snow, but the real carpets of flowers emerge in July and August.

A patented view, a hallmark of Lake Louise – the red poppies in manicured gardens along the Lake. The site is visited by thousands of people daily. Early explorer Tom Wilson discovered it in 1882; the Lake is named after Princess Louise, a daughter of Queen Victoria. Lake Louise is 1735m above sea level and its yearly average water temperature is from 1-5°C. The length is 2.4 km, width 1km, and depth circa 80m.

JASPER NATIONAL PARK

Jasper Park is another shining diamond of the Rocky Mountain National Parks – pristine, green, natural, the 'real thing' - as a national park should be. It is easy to access from south, east and west by well-maintained highways and by rail. The Town of Jasper is friendly, cozy and offers first-class accommodation, facilities and services. This is the Park where one can see wildlife and unspoiled nature at a slow pace. The Park offers numerous spectacular destinations to visit by car, horseback, boat, or by hiking. At the south end of the Park may be found the world famous Columbia Icefield, a solid sheet of ice, 325 sq. km, with five major glaciers and 14 mountains exceeding 11,000 feet/3,350m. Mt. Columbia (3,747m) the second highest in the Rockies, is readily accessible to, well-equipped and experienced mountaineers, year round. Nearby Mt. Alberta (3,619m) is another story – a few people attempt to climb it each year but only the top guns succeed. West of the Columbia Icefield sprawls equally large Clemenceau Icefield, together they form the largest body of ice in the Rockies. Interesting is the Mt. Fryatt Group and closer to Jasper, Mt. Edith Cavell (3,363m), a known attraction accessible by a winding mountain road. West of Cavell, a major hiking trail leads to Tonquin Valley, another shining jewel of the Park. Two Amethyst Lakes, the spectacularly jagged The Ramparts, and resident Grizzly, Caribou, and Wolf, make it a "must see" area. But...you have seen nothing until you see Maligne Lake, accessible by a paved road southeast of the Town of Jasper. Here the mountains are lofty and of stark beauty, the water is clear and blue, emanating from numerous glaciers and Brazeau Icefield. Moose, Grizzly, and Caribou, are year-round residents here as well. Recently a pack of Wolves took up residence, making a good living in the wildlife-rich Valley. Paddling a canoe to the end of this 22 km long lake and camping there offers an experience that can 'easily' be done in five or six hours.

Another unique phenomenon is Medicine Lake on the same road. In the early summer when snow and ice melt water is pouring into the lake, the water level is high, but come autumn when the water slows to a trickle, the lake virtually disappears. The underground channels drain the water away and Moose have no place to escape predators. On his last visit in autumn, the author has seen a large gathering of Wolves squabbling over Moose filet mignon on the other side of the dry lake. Sad, but this is nature's way!

Miette Hot Springs, in the northeast part of the Park, is another attraction worth visiting. Close to the Town of Jasper, a number of picturesque lakes dot the land: Patricia and Pyramid Lakes next to the local landmark, Pyramid Mountain (2,766m), are the best known. The northwesterly portion of the Park is extremely wild and not easily accessible. There along Snake Indian River, a large waterfall is located, but the return hike is about 50 km. The northern perimeter borders Willmore Wilderness Park and Mt. Robson Provincial Park (west side) where the monarch of the Rockies – Mt. Robson (3,954m) reaches sky high. Jasper Park offers many major hiking trails allowing deep penetration into real wilderness areas; many equipped with campgrounds. Winter is a time when nature takes a break and snoozes cozily under a fluffy blanket of snow. However, most of the animals and skiers do not hibernate. Cross-country skiing enthusiasts can find unlimited terrain to explore and alpine skiers can schuss to their heart's content at the great Marmot Ski Area. The Park's wildlife is basically the same as listed in Banff Park. If you appreciate unspoiled wilderness, peace, freedom of the hills and quest for adventure, Jasper Park is the place to find it all.

From snowy Mt. Fryatt to icy Mt. Edith Cavell sprawls a great pristine boreal forest.

The Global Perspective: As world population spins out of control and doubles every 50 years or so, the land does not increase, which means we have less and less space in which to live. Water shortages are already apparent, food deficits are quickly approaching, and new deadly diseases keep cropping up, so quality of life is dropping rapidly everywhere. Desperate attempts are being made to save green spaces from destruction but efforts are hampered by ever-hungry industries which will gladly cut down every last tree to make just one more dollar. A few enlightened nations can see clearly what is coming and are trying to create as many National Parks as they can afford. Canada being so huge, and with such a small population, could easily afford to be a world leader in the National Park concept. There are, however, countries that have no national parks to speak of. Some large countries have only two to three percent in area designated to parks. Ten percent of the land mass of each country should be given to green lands. Some countries have already exceeded that percentage voluntarily to 20% (Cuba 22%). The time is coming when industrial wastes, air pollution, and toxins, will render water non-drinkable, and food inedible. Only then will the world come to realize that drastic change is needed or the whole eco-system will collapse. Since in the last 60 years more damage has been caused to the environment than in the past 1,000 years, clearly mankind is capable of destroying the entire planet in the next 100 years. The problem is that people always wake up too late. Friends, the ecological alarm clock is running. Will we wake up? What do we do? Let's set standards: each country must set aside 15% of its land for national parks, thereby contributing to the global fresh air bank. Reduce population through responsible family planning. Have utmost respect for all green things – this is essential for health and life. Plant trees; green is health; the concrete jungle is cancer. Recycle. Mountains of garbage will one day overwhelm us. Buy only what you need and consume what you buy thereby decreasing waste and pollution. Do we really need paper cups, lids and straws for our drinks and three napkins at each meal? If we all did our part, our ecology would recover and survive. It is up to each one of us. Do your part!

Above: The pearl of Jasper National Park, the blue-green Maligne Lake. This 22km long jewel features tremendous ice-capped mountains, countless scenic quiet bays-coves, and islands. Fauna represented here are Moose, Caribou, the odd Elk, Deer, Bear, and Wolf, plus several smaller species. Low temperatures as a result of the high altitude, the presence of numerous glaciers, and Brazeau Icefield, prevent flora from flourishing.

Left: Whoever knows the Rockies must have heard about the legendary beauty of Spirit Island on Maligne Lake, and a beauty it is! On a warm, long, sunny summer day, take a canoe and in three hours you are there. Another three hours will get you to Coronet Creek, the Lake's end. Camp here, take a hike to Coronet Glacier, and voila – great adventure is yours. Be prepared however, because this beautiful lake can turn stormy, ugly and dangerous, on short notice.

Above: This is Tonquin Valley located west of Mt. Edith Cavell. The Valley features two Amethyst Lakes, source of Astoria River. The Ramparts, an incredibly rugged but beautiful Range area, has endless flowery meadows and some smaller trees as the Valley is at treeline. Regardless high altitude and northern latitude flowers here are lush and of great variety, including blue lupines. This is Grizzly country, who also share this paradise with small herd of Mountain Caribou and a few other mammals.

Left: Northwest of Sunwapta Pass along Icefields Parkway, the landscape resembles more moonscape than Rockies, featuring rock, gravel, silty moraines, and not much else. Here and there, however, large clusters of flowers manage to cling to this harsh reality. West of Mt. Athabasca (3490m) on sheltered flats along the Sunwapta River, a great colony of Willow Herb (Epilobium latifolium) finds a suitable habitat, common on wet sandy-gravelled river bars. Circumpolar, arctic-alpine.

In the south-central part of the Park along Endless Chain Range nestles picturesque Honeymoon Lake, a pretty, serene, place with a small campground, ideal for a short relaxing get-away. In any direction, spectacular wilderness sprawls, surrounded by endless forest and majestic mountains.

Athabasca River began at the Columbia Icefield's Columbia Glacier, and cut through most of the south central part of the Park. The photo features the area south of Mt. Kerkeslin where high, exposed cliffs contain many minerals vital to animals. On a good day, if you are lucky, you may see 20 Goats and a few Elk here.

Above: In the lower valleys spring has arrived in early May; on higher mountains, snow will linger for another month or longer. The Whistlers (2466m) on the left, Indian Ridge and Muhigan Mountain, all reflect their snowy faces in Pyramid Lake located just five kilometers north of Jasper, as the crow flies.

Left: Maligne Lake may be reached by a scenic drive 48 km southeast of Jasper. Winter remains here for seven months because of high elevation of 1690m, while the Town of Jasper (elevation 1063m) enjoys a much shorter winter. At the Lake's outlet, ice melts first, allowing newly-arrived waterfowl to cool off after the long flight from the hot south.

Above: The majestic dweller of the north, Moose Cow (Alces alces) proudly shows off her new winter coat, while looking attentively at her male friend hidden in the dense bush. Moose population is declining in direct proportion to the increase of development and human activities. In the remote north, Moose are faring well.

Left: Mighty in the summer, Athabasca River looks quite meager in late September as water is scarce. Spectacular Athabasca Falls plunges deep into a gorge carved through the ages by swift water. Since the water originates at the Columbia Icefield, its water is silt-laden, resulting in its green hue.

Upper: There are never enough photos of glorious Maligne Lake. Late afternoon light reveals the gentle beauty of the Lake and Mt. Charlton (3217m) on the left, and Mt. Unwin (3268m). Summer at its best by the Lake which offers so much beauty and activities.

Lower: Autumnish glorious colours of Athabasca River Valley, just southeast of the Town of Jasper. September and October are mostly dry and sunny. Summer crowds are gone and the big rush is over so for those who can take a week or two to be here will certainly enjoy great fun.

Left: The mystery of Medicine Lake unfolds again in late autumn. As summer meltwater is very scarce, the Lake's water drains through underground channels and by November, the Lake is entirely gone. Moose are deprived of the safety of the water and often fall victim to hungry wolf packs.

A known landmark of the Jasper area, Pyramid Mountain (2766m) reflects its craggy southeastern face in peaceful Patricia Lake. To attain a blue sky morning, golden hues of poplar, and quiet, non-windy weather, is simply good luck and a great reward for a patient and persistent photographer.

Just north of Maligne Lake, a hiking trail allows a visit to interesting rolling hills above the treeline called Opal Hills. Elevation gain is nearly 500m so plan on four hours for a round trip. This high tundra is extremely fragile – please use trail only. Charlton-Unwin Massif looms on the left.

Above: It is the end of July and Elk antlers are still growing. A rich menu of mountain meadows provides all the minerals required to grow these enormous racks which Bull Elk (Cervus canadensis) use to defeat competitors in autumn rutting battles and as a defense against critters who try to make a meal of him!

Left: Mt. Kerkeslin (2956m) dominates the Athabasca Valley near Athabasca Falls. The mountain is a year-round home to a large colony of Mountain Goat which often wander down to river cliffs rich in minerals. The photo features the west face reflected in a small tarn; north slopes are entirely covered by a large body of ice.

Above: A different image of Athabasca Falls, or rather a portion of it. The sun was very low in the western sky casting an interesting light on this pure clear water. Time exposure allowed for the veiled effect. It is not recommended to get too close to the rushing water as the rock is wet and extremely slippery causing death to 'brave' souls almost every year.

Left: Another two hours of hard scramble gets one to the peak (2790m) north of Opal Hills. Looking west, endless peaks of Queen Elizabeth and Colin Ranges sweep the horizon. Above the climber, Opal Peak rises sharply, dusted by the first autumn snow. It is a great feeling to be on top of any mountain – would you try? In the hidden valley west of Opal Hills, one may spot a Grizzly or Mountain Caribou.

A small quiet cove in Pyramid Lake north of Jasper allowed this moody artistic photo to be created. In the Jasper region, along both sides of the broad Athabasca River valley, dozens of lakes of various size are scattered. Pyramid is the largest, then Patricia, Riley, Mina, Cabin, Marjore, Hibernia and Caledonia. East of the river: Lake Edith, Annette, and Beauvert, to name a few.

Mt. Edith Cavell (3363m) is a lofty Jasper area landmark of stark beauty and a renowned climbing site. The fearsome north face route requires an entire day, if all goes well, or one face bivouac on an icy wall. The author is not so adventurous, so he took the much easier south face route five times, never having decent enough weather to create great photos. The wise and happy folks take it easy – never mind north or south face!

Above: A group of avid canoeists just completed a little outing, paddling along the mighty Athabasca River northeast of Jasper. Canoeing, kayaking or sailing, are as Canadian as hockey or an igloo. The great outdoors is healthy and fun, and the more the better.

Left: Just north of Jasper along Snaring River, a great wetland and marshes sprawl (photo) joining Jasper Lake. Snake Indian River nearby is draining the very remote and wild north part of the Park. Backpacking there is still a great exotic adventure, seldom found elsewhere.

Above: As tradition in pictorial book calls for the last photo to be of a sunset, here we see half-dry Medicine Lake channels in late autumn illuminated by a mysterious alpine glow. The real sunset over Cottonwood Slough just north of Jasper (left) appears redder than it should? Yes, this is due to ashes in the air from numerous forest fires which plagued the west in the summer of 2003. These fires lasted for three months which prevented taking nature photography, but permitted a few spectacular sunset photos.

The Author

The creator of this modest but interesting album is a man in love with his subject – the Canadian Rockies – a lifelong affair.

George always loved nature and its soothing magical powers, so he greatly enjoys serenity and peace in the midst of the Canadian Rockies. George is a mountain man; he hikes, scrambles, climbs, and explores mountain wilderness – always with camera at ready. He has climbed over 400 mountains, published 35 pictorial books and developed a lifelong strong special relationship with the mountains, so the rigors and hardship of mountaineering is enjoyable to him. He is a kind of masochist so pain is an integral part of his daily life. No pain, no gain!

Joining the Boy Scouts at the age of seven guided his life in the right direction and now his activities and publishing influences generations of young Canadians who follow in his footsteps. One can either go to a smoky bar or to the quiet, inspiring and beautiful mountains.

George is an avid environmentalist who believes as Henry D. Thoreau did that, "In wilderness is the preservation of the world". He has planted over 3000 trees to make our increasingly gray world a shade greener and healthier. Would you follow his example? Plant a few trees on your property or sponsor tree planting programs. Have a wilderness in your backyard!

Photographic Studies by George Brybycin :
The High Rockies
Colourful Calgary
Our Fragile Wilderness
The Rocky Mountains
Banff National Park
Jasper National Park
Colourful Calgary II
Wildlife in the Rockies
Rocky Mountain Symphony
Enchanted Wilderness
Wilderness Odyssey
Rocky Mountain Symphony II
Romance of the Rockies
Calgary - The Sunshine City
The Living Rockies
Cosmopolitan Calgary
Banff and Jasper N.P.
The Rockies: Wildlife
The Majestic Rockies
Emerald Waters of the Rockies
The Canadian Rockies Panoramas
Eternal Rockies
Calgary, the Stampede City and Environs
Alpine Meadows
The Rockies, British Columbia, The North
Rocky Mountain Odyssey
Banff & Jasper National Parks II
The Canadian Rockies
The Canadian Rockies Panoromas II
The Pristine Rockies
Calgary, Pearl of The West
The Rockies, Living Waters
The Grand Canadian Rockies
The Green & Wild Canadian Rockies
Banff & Jasper - The Splendid National Parks

Front Cover: Upper Waterfowl Lake, Banff National Park
Back Cover: Maligne Lake, Jasper National Park

This book was created in Alberta by Albertans
Printed in China by Everbest Printing Co.
Text Editor: Helen Turgeon
Design: George Brybycin
Typeseting: K & H United Co.
Colour Separations: Precision Colour Imaging
First Edition: 2004

ISBN 0-919029-35-3

This is George Brybycin's 35th book.

For current list, please write to:

GB PUBLISHING, Box 6292, Station D,
Calgary, Alberta Canada T2P 2C9

"In wilderness is the preservation of the world."

George Brybycin's collection of 15,000 35mm colour slides is FOR SALE at nominal price.
Subjects include: The Rockies, Western and Northern Canada, Calgary, The 1988 Olympics, Alaska, The Western U.S. and the World (Paris, London). Also available is the collection of all 35 George's books. Offers may be tendered to GB Publishing at the address above.